ideals®
MOTHER'S DAY

More Than 50 Years of Celebrating Life's Most Treasured Moments

Vol. 56, No. 2

"Mother is the name for God in the lips
and hearts of little children."

—William Makepeace Thackeray

IDEALS—Vol. 56, No. 2 March MCMXCIX IDEALS (ISSN 0019-137X) is published six
times a year: January, March, May, July, September, and November by
IDEALS PUBLICATIONS INCORPORATED,
535 Metroplex Drive, Suite 250, Nashville, TN 37211.
Periodical postage paid at Nashville, Tennessee, and additional mailing offices.
Copyright © MCMXCIX by IDEALS PUBLICATIONS INCORPORATED.
POSTMASTER: Send address changes to Ideals, PO Box 305300,
Nashville, TN 37230. All rights reserved.
Title IDEALS registered U.S. Patent Office.

SINGLE ISSUE—U.S. $5.95 USD; Higher in Canada
ONE-YEAR SUBSCRIPTION—U.S. $19.95 USD; Canada $36.00 CDN (incl. GST and shipping); Foreign $25.95 USD
TWO-YEAR SUBSCRIPTION—U.S. $35.95 USD; Canada $66.50 CDN (incl. GST and shipping); Foreign $47.95 USD

ISBN 0-8249-1154-7   GST 131903775

Cover Photo
Springtime in the Garden
Photo by
Nancy Matthews

Inside Covers
VEGETABLE GARDEN, TRELLIS WORK
Charles Neal, artist
Superstock

A Waking World

Stella Craft Tremble

Lashing winds have ceased their blowing,
Now the time for garden sowing.
Tiny shoots are upward growing—
Spring is yawning in her sleep.

Yellow daffodils are peeping
From the sod where they were sleeping;
Memory bells from heart's safekeeping
Ring of daisy blooms, knee-deep.

Trillium push their dainty faces
Up through hidden marshy places;
Pink arbutus lend their graces
To the woodland where they creep.

Safe, unharmed by cold distresses,
All the tulips don gay dresses,
And the alder shakes her tresses
Near the stream where willows weep.

Mockingbirds and wrens are singing,
Phoebes from the south are winging
While renascent spring is bringing
Joy to all, profound and deep.

*A field of lupine and columbine welcome the morning in
Vashon Island, Washington. Photo by Mary Liz Austin.*

EARTH'S FRAGRANCE

Edna Jaques

I love the blessed fragrance of the spring—
The smell of sod rising into the air,
Moist loam and furrows steaming in the sun,
Fragrant as lily buds, and everywhere
Little green noses pushing up the sod
Like tiny scouts before a marching squad.

The lowlands have a fragrance of their own,
Of melted snow, wet twigs, and drying boughs;
Warm hollows where the grass is faintly green,
The call of birds who follow after plows,
Wheeling and dipping in a maze of flight
From barn to field and back in sheer delight.

There is the odor of wild cherry bloom,
Trillium and dogwood, violets faintly sweet,
The taste of alders on the morning wind,
The earthy smell of newly sprouted wheat,
Old rotting logs, fresh willows in a clump,
The smell of moss by an old hickory stump.

The spongy odor of a nearby bog,
Bloodroot and wintergreen, the scent of pine
Stretching its eager limbs to find the sun
With every leaf and twig a weather sign.
Knowing all this if I were blind and dumb,
I know my heart would tell me spring had come.

Brilliant azaleas and trees adorned with Spanish moss epitomize springtime in Charleston, South Carolina. Photo by Superstock.

From My Garden Journal

by Deana Deck

DIANTHUS AND ARTEMISIA

In myth, folklore, and fairy tales, plants are often symbols for heroes and heroines, gods and goddesses. The plants dianthus (commonly known as the carnation) and artemisia (also called wormwood) both derive their names from a Greek myth of star-crossed lovers. In this myth, the Greek goddess Dianthus and her beloved, the Greek god Artemisia, are transformed into the plants that now bear their names.

According to Greek mythology, Artemisia was the only son of Artemis, who was the daughter of Zeus and the goddess and protector of young women. Dianthus, known as the "divine flower," was a favorite of Artemis. She was a beautiful young goddess who, against the advice of her elders, came to earth disguised as a shepherdess to experience human life. When the handsome Artemisia saw her, he was overwhelmed by her beauty and pursued her. Dianthus returned his love, but Artemisia later abandoned her and returned to his home. Perhaps this is why in the language of herbs, *artemisia* means absence.

Dianthus followed him, desperately pleading for his return. Artemisia agreed, but his mother, enraged that her son had deserted the beautiful young maiden, sentenced him to death. When Dianthus discovered his body, she killed herself and threw her body onto his. Their blood mingled in the soil, and two plants emerged. One was the bitter wormwood, artemisia; the other was the sweet carnation, dianthus. Seeing the two together, Artemis repented and forgave the young lovers. Mixing a potion from the two plants, she restored her son and his "divine flower" to life.

It's impossible to know which of the many varieties of artemisia grew out of the legend, but two types, wormwood and mugwort, were used medicinally in older times to treat illnesses such as epilepsy.

DIANTHUS ✦ ARTEMISIA

In modern gardens, several species are popular, including one known as Silver Mound, which grows well in rock gardens. Much like the other species of artemisia, its leaves are silvery-gray and feathery and contrast nicely with the darker foliage of sedums, another popular rock garden plant. The Silver King variety of artemisia grows to about two feet in height and is lovely in a perennial border, since it keeps its foliage all winter in mild climates. It is also easy to dry and adds a nice silver accent to dried arrangements. Two popular plants, the dusty miller and the desert sagebrush, are other types of artemisia, as is the herb tarragon.

The dianthus, which was known to the ancient Greeks as "divine flower," symbolizes divine love in the language of flowers. It is best known to the modern world as the carnation. There are dozens of types of dianthus, some annual, some biennial, and some perennial. The best known are the biennial sweet william (*D. barbatus*); the greenhouse carnation (*D. caryophyllus*), which blooms year round; and the diminutive cottage pink

(*D. plumerius*), which is a perennial favorite in the garden.

Dianthus is one of the few flowering garden plants that prefers a somewhat alkaline soil. This may be how it came to be associated with artemisia, legends not withstanding. Artemisia can be found growing wild near deserts, which are usually of a more alkaline soil. Hence, the plants seem to prefer similar growing conditions. However, the ability artemisia has to grow in the desert is a testament to the plant's hardiness, which surpasses that of the dianthus.

This May, I plan to combine dried or fresh dianthus and artemisia with sheet moss and clusters of thyme, marjoram, and boxwood to form small herbal wreaths. These will be perfect for gift-giving. Just for fun, I'll add a card relating the tragic myth of young Artemisia and Dianthus. What better reminder could there be of the power of love than these legendary flowers?

Small herbal wreaths made of dried or fresh dianthus, artemisia, sheet moss, and clusters of thyme, marjoram, and boxwood are perfect for gift-giving, particularly on Mother's Day.

Deana Deck tends to her flowers, plants, and vegetables at her home in Nashville, Tennessee, where her popular garden column is a regular feature in The Tennessean.

His Wondrous Works

Kay Hoffman

How can one say there is no God
When everywhere we've looked or trod
His wondrous works on every hand
Defy our minds to understand?

The changing seasons, come what may,
The moon, the stars, the sun's bright ray;
A little child with laughing eyes,
A newborn baby's soft, low cry.

Wildflowers blooming by the road
Where no man e'er had his abode;
A robin singing in the rain
That bids us praise God's holy name.

The ocean waves, the ebb and flow,
The beauty of fresh-fallen snow;
Small furry folk along the lane
Where maple trees wear scarlet flame.

He who proclaims there is no God
Must not have seen these things we laud.
The heavens, earth, the restless sea
All tell us of His majesty.

Overleaf photo: Common camas and western buttercup blanket a field in the Columbia River Gorge National Scenic Area in Washington. Photo by Mary Liz Austin.

Left: The wonders of the season cover this wisteria vine and hawthorn tree in Multnomah County, Oregon. Photo by Steve Terrill Photography.

FROM THE SECRET GARDEN

Frances Hodgson Burnett

One of the nice little gusts of wind rushed down the walk, and it was a stronger one than the rest. It was strong enough to wave the branches of the trees, and it was more than strong enough to sway the trailing sprays of untrimmed ivy hanging from the wall. Mary had stepped close to the robin, and suddenly the gust of wind swung aside some loose ivy trails, and more suddenly still she jumped toward it and caught it in her hand. This she did because she had seen something under it—a round knob which had been covered by the leaves hanging over it. It was the knob of a door.

She put her hands under the leaves and began to pull and push them aside. Thick as the ivy hung, it nearly all was a loose and swinging curtain, though some had crept over wood and iron. Mary's heart began to thump and her hands to shake a little in her delight and excitement. . . . What was this under her hands which was square and made of iron and which her fingers found a hole in? It was the lock of the door which had been closed ten years and she put her hand in her pocket, drew out the key and found it fitted the keyhole. She put the key in and turned it. It took two hands to do it, but it did turn.

And then she took a long breath . . . and pushed back the swinging curtain of ivy and pushed back the door which opened slowly—slowly. Then she slipped through it, and shut it behind her, and stood with her back against it, looking about her and breathing quite fast with excitement, and wonder, and delight. She was standing *inside* the secret garden. It was the sweetest, most mysterious-looking place anyone could imagine.

The high walls which shut it in were covered with the leafless stems of climbing roses, which were so thick that they were matted together. Mary Lennox knew they were roses because she had seen a great many roses in India. All the ground was covered with grass of wintry brown, and out of it grew clumps of bushes which were surely rose-bushes if they were alive. There were numbers of standard roses which had so spread their branches that they were like little trees. There were other trees in the garden, and one of the things that made the place look strangest and loveliest was that climbing roses had run all over them and swung down long tendrils which made light swaying curtains, and here and there they had caught at each other or at a far-reaching branch and had crept from one tree to another and made lovely bridges of themselves. There were neither leaves nor roses on them now, and Mary did not know whether they were dead or alive, but their thin grey or brown branches and sprays looked like a sort of hazy mantle spreading over everything, walls, and trees, and even brown grass, where they had fallen from their fastenings, and run along the ground. It was this hazy tangle from tree to tree which made it all look so mysterious.

Mary had thought it must be different from other gardens which had not been left all by themselves so long; and, indeed, it was different from any other place she had ever seen in her life . . . and she felt as if she had found a world all her own.

a promise of beauty full-blown and free!

This not-so-secret rose garden in Cape Cod, Massachusetts, shares its beauty with passers-by. Photo by William Johnson/Johnson's Photography.

vision of things that are to be!

Phyllis C. Michael

Not Far from Eden

Cecelia Gustin

Oh, I remember dimly purple hills
　　That rimmed the flowering meadowland,
The cottonwoods that spread their cooling shade
　　Above rye fields and strips of gleaming sand.
There, cattle drowsed and lazed in afternoon,
　　And blackbirds swung on gently swaying weeds.
Wild berries ripened under heavy boughs,
　　And dandelions cast their errant seeds.

Peace had its reign there all day long.
　　The farmer came with garden spade and hoe
And turned fresh sod to meet the warming sun
　　Till shadows lengthened under evening's glow.
The feeding birds by twos and threes took flight,
　　And playful little lambs came home at night!

A stream holds springtime waters in this scene in Pickens County,
South Carolina. Photo by William Johnson/Johnson's Photography.

Moonlight and Honeysuckle

How fitting and appropriate for Mother's Day are the fragrance and loveliness of the honeysuckle. When the blooms reach their prime in the warmth of spring, they form garlands along the roadsides and transform the hedges and banks into gardens of scented beauty. The vibrant honeysuckle thrives in thickets and hedges and forms mounds of blossoms over old stumps and stone walls.

I have often walked in the sun to enjoy the loveliness and sweetness of the bloom. Now and then I continue walking into the night to enjoy the aromas the dark hours bring. The dew of evening seems to freshen the fragrance that fills the air. The moisture settles the dust of day, clearing and cleansing the atmosphere and making far richer the delicate aroma of the flowers. Where the bees hummed and worked among the flowers in the sunlit hours, only a soothing quietness remains under the glow of a soft and mellow moon and the twinkling stars above.

For a week of nights I walked the same familiar road, breathing in the sweetness of the honeysuckle, the sweetness of the spring. I was unwilling to miss a moment of the fragrance and unwilling to give up the golden light of the Maytime moon as it illuminated the banks and roadsides, like the light of a lantern shining on honeysuckle blooms.

The author of two published books, Lansing Christman has been contributing to Ideals *for more than twenty years. Mr. Christman has also been published in several American, foreign, and braille anthologies. He lives in rural South Carolina.*

Honeysuckle scampers over the landscape in Lancaster County, Pennsylvania. Photo by William Johnson/Johnson's Photography.

Little House

Sudie Stuart Hager

Nature must love a little house,

Else why does she, in spring,

Border it with hyacinths

And urge its wren to sing?

She drapes its summer trellises

With roses, all they'll hold;

In fall she lays upon its porch

A mat of pure leaf gold.

And even when winter comes to stay,

With iciness and storm,

She wraps that house in feather quilts

To keep it snug and warm.

A stone wall borders the garden at this little house in Waldoboro, Maine. Photo by Dianne Dietrich Leis.

CLOUDS

Mary Cates

Thanks for clouds with moisture laden
In the sky of purest blue,
Variant as a youthful maiden,
Fleeting as the morning dew.

Lofty clouds that touch the rafters
Of the universe so wild,
Then a small one trailing after
Like a lagging, errant child.

One by one in swift succession,
Silent, soft upon the breeze,
With a purpose seem to press on
Over mountains, plains, and seas.

Matchless show of splendid beauty
Massing in their ranks on high,
Racing off to some far duty
In a dark and stormy sky.

Streaked with brilliant shades of color
Both at dawning and at eve;
Changing, darkening, growing duller,
What a tapestry they weave.

Lord, I thank You with elation
For the gift of clouds above—
Wondrous act of Your creation,
Gift of beauty and of love.

A wing-like cloud floats above this golden field of flowers in Bavaria, Germany. Photo by Superstock.

Touched by a light that hath no name,
A glory never sung,
Aloft on sky and mountain wall
Are God's great pictures hung.
—John Greenleaf Whittier

The Humble-Bee

Ralph Waldo Emerson

Photo by Neal Mishler/FPG International.

Burly, dozing humble-bee,
Where thou art is clime for me.
Let them sail for Porto Rique,
Far-off heats through seas to seek;
I will follow thee alone,
Thou animated torrid-zone!
Zigzag steerer, desert cheerer,
Let me chase thy waving lines;
Keep me nearer, me thy hearer,
Singing over shrubs and vines.

Insect lover of the sun,
Joy of thy dominion!
Sailor of the atmosphere;
Swimmer through the waves of air;
Voyager of light and noon;
Epicurean of June;
Wait, I prithee, till I come
Within earshot of thy hum—
All without is martyrdom.

When the south wind, in May days,
With a net of shining haze
Silvers the horizon wall,
And with softness touching all

Tints the human countenance
With a color of romance,
And infusing subtle heats,
Turns the sod to violets,
Thou, in sunny solitudes,
Rover of the underwoods,
The green silence dost displace
With thy mellow, breezy bass.

Hot midsummer's petted crone,
Sweet to me thy drowsy tone
Tells of countless sunny hours,
Long days, and solid banks of flowers;
Of gulfs of sweetness without bound
In Indian wildernesses found;
Of Syrian peace, immortal leisure,
Firmest cheer, and bird-like pleasure.

Aught unsavory or unclean
Hath my insect never seen;
But violets and bilberry bells,
Maple-sap and daffodels,
Grass with green flag half-mast high,
Succory to match the sky,
Columbine with horn of honey,
Scented fern, and agrimony,
Clover, catchfly, adder's-tongue
And brier-roses, dwelt among;
All beside was unknown waste,
All was picture as he passed.

Wiser far than human seer,
Yellow-breeched philosopher!
Seeing only what is fair,
Sipping only what is sweet,
Thou dost mock at fate and care,
Leave the chaff, and take the wheat.
When the fierce northwestern blast
Cools sea and land so far and fast,
Thou already slumberest deep;
Woe and want thou canst outsleep;
Want and woe, which torture us,
Thy sleep makes ridiculous.

Nature

Emily Dickinson

Nature—the Gentlest Mother is,
    Impatient of no Child—
The feeblest—or the waywardest—
    Her Admonition mild—

In Forest—and the Hill—
    By Traveller— be heard—
Restraining Rampant Squirrel—
    Or too impetuous Bird—

How fair Her Conversation—
    A Summer Afternoon—
Her Household—Her Assembly—
    And when the Sun go down—

Her Voice among the Aisles
    Incite the timid prayer
Of the minutest Cricket—
    The most unworthy Flower—

When all the Children sleep—
    She turns as long away
As will suffice to light Her lamps—
    Then bending from the Sky—

With infinite Affection—
    And infiniter Care—
Her Golden finger on Her lip—
    Wills Silence—Everywhere—

Above: A sleeping newborn smiles, dreaming.
Photo by Stephanie Rausser/FPG International.

Left: Meadow grasses lean toward the setting sun in
Livermore, New Hampshire. Photo by William
Johnson/Johnson's Photography.

Maternal Song

Sudie Stuart Hager

How can I tell of a mother's worth?
By a song of the all-sustaining earth;
The earth that watches young plants rise
With arms outstretched to the distant skies;
The earth that gives them zeal to grow,
But keeps their eager roots in tow;
That urges them to stand up proud,
Sustains them when their heads are bowed,
And strengthens them to face again
The thrusts of wind and hail and rain,
So they may bloom, bear fruit and seed
To meet the hungering, tired world's need.

I sing of the kindly, nurturing earth
To tell of a mother's priceless worth.

Readers' Reflections

Editor's Note: Readers are invited to submit unpublished, original poetry for possible publication in future issues of Ideals. Please send typed copies only; manuscripts will not be returned. Writers receive $10 for each published submission. Send material to Readers' Reflections, Ideals Publications, Inc., P.O. Box 305300, Nashville, Tennessee 37230-5300.

Love

Love is a lilac-scented flower in a field of daisies
    in the springtime.
Love is a kind remark on a dreary winter day
    to cheer someone in a special way.
Love is a present, unexpected, small,
    in its own pricelessness.
Love is a child come to say hello
    to a friend on a summer day.

Love is the sun's rays on the window.
Love is an ancient friendship starting over again.
Love is God's child knocking on the door.

Ashley Williams
Lexington, Kentucky

A Mother and Her Child

A lovely face, a melody,
A flower sweet and fair
Are some of life's most treasured gifts,
Both beautiful and rare.

But fingers ne'er could capture,
No matter how they tried,
To put upon a canvas
A mother and her child.

Your picture will be lovelier
Than any I could see.
And so as motherhood draws nigh,
I make my prayer for thee,

That God in all His mercy,
So tender and so mild,
Will bless and keep you in His care,
Dear mother and your child.

Regina Scopelitis
Tucson, Arizona

A Mother's Gift

What child is this with eyes so blue
That God has given me
To love and cherish through the years
For all the world to see?

Sometimes I feel unworthy;
For all I have to give
Is the very essence of my soul,
A deep yearning to live,
To live a life that's rich and full

And share with you its glory,
To love and comfort you, my child,
As life unfolds its story.

I'll comfort and enfold you
Until it's time to send
You soaring on life's currents,
Your own life to transcend.

Linda Corkery
Staatsburg, New York

Come, Come

"Come, come," called Mother's voice
In gentle lilting air;
"Come, come," repeated childish tones
In sweetness, oh, so fair.

Then from the other room she came
With tiny, tripping tread;
For she had found her mother's shoes,
Which had been 'neath the bed.

Mother smiled with twinkling eyes;
"My precious darling dear,
Those shoes you wear are thrice the size
You normally would wear."

The tiny face shone much with joy;
And though the words she couldn't say,
It seemed her eyes so sweetly said,
"I'll be like you someday."

So tender sweet the moment
As the two of them stood there;
Then Mother knelt beside her girl
And kissed her with a prayer.

"Oh, Father God," she whispered soft,
"You've lent this child a time;
Please guide my steps to walk Your way,
For her steps follow mine.

"And make my errors to be few;
That with my closing tread,
Regrets in number shall be small
In what I've done and said.

"If I can but her steps guide right
I shan't have walked in vain.
And when my life one day is o'er,
I know we'll meet again."

The tiny child with tilted head
Returned her mother's kiss.
"Come, come," re-echoed childish words
With trusting, loving lips.

Gail Elizabeth Newcomb
Aurora, Colorado

Collecting Dandelions, Collecting Memories

Maria Brady-Smith

It is spring. I'm not sure why, but this year, I am more keenly aware of the changes around me. Every day, I see something new blooming in the yard or another tiny green sprout that the sun has coaxed out of the ground. The redbuds in our yard are brilliant. The phlox and bluebells, dogwood and lilac bushes are all heavenly in their beauty. The forsythia and daffodils and jonquils have already come and gone.

But my favorites are the dandelions. Yes, dandelions. They spot our yard like freckles on a young girl's face. I would never think of getting rid of them, because dandelions are the picking flowers. You see, I have three daughters, and there is something about little girls and flower picking.

My two oldest daughters are way beyond that. At fourteen and eleven, their hands are busy applying fingernail polish, practicing the piano, and dribbling basketballs. But not Grace. She's three, a magical age—she *is* springtime.

On a beautiful sunny day, she floats down the front steps in her favorite dress, the wind blowing her hair. She dances and skips through the yard as if she were called by some mysterious music that I long ago stopped hearing. She spots a robin pecking for a worm. Quietly, she stalks him, ever hopeful that she will catch him this time. Of course, he startles and flies away long before she can get near him. But she is not too disappointed, because suddenly she has caught a whiff of the lilac bush and quickly sticks her nose among the blooms.

She crouches down to observe something on the ground a little more closely. I get back to my reading on the porch, content that my child is happily entertaining herself. A few minutes later, I look up to see her on the steps, holding her hand behind her back.

"I have a surprise for you," she says in a sing-song voice. I put my book down and meet her at the top of the steps.

"What is it?" I ask, mocking anticipation.

"Close your eyes," she insists.

I close my eyes momentarily; and when I open them, I do have a big surprise. There in front of me is the face of an angel, looking up at me with eyes so full of love and pride that I can feel the breath go out of me. In her tight fist is a clump of already wilting dandelions.

"Oh, Grace," I say, "They are so beautiful. Thank you." And I really mean that. They are the most beautiful thing I can imagine right now, a gift of love from a three-year-old child. My mind wanders back to two other small girls who gave me similar gifts of love, and I wonder where the time has gone. I wish that I could keep this moment forever. If only I could just pluck it out of time and press it in a book so that I could pull it back out in twenty years and feel it again, complete. But I know now that I can't do that. So I lean down and give her a warm hug and kiss, and we walk into our house together, in search of the perfect vase.

Common dandelions mingle with phlox in Grant County, Wisconsin. Photo by Terry Donnelly.

Gifts from the Heart

Myrtle Vorst Sheppard

Last year John gave me perfume,
And Paul an amethyst,
And Ann showered me with roses.
But oh, the very best
Of their fine grown-up presents
Could only half compare
With all the little bygone gifts
My heart keeps finding there
Within its deep recesses,
Its secret memory room.
Still glistening with the morning dew
Is sweet Ann's chain of clover bloom.
And two round stones that Paul gave me
Are still as red and sleek
And precious as the day
He found them by the creek.
John honored me with crawdads,
Ferocious, whiskered fellows.
The three of them brought blossoms
In gaudy reds and yellows.
Oh, adult gifts are lovely;
They make the teardrops start.
But how small, childish offerings
Touch a mother's heart!

A young boy presents a gift to his mother along Boston's Esplanade. Photo by Dianne Dietrich Leis.

Devotions FROM THE Heart

Pamela Kennedy

She openeth her mouth with wisdom; and in her tongue is the law of kindness.
Proverbs 31:26

WISDOM AND KINDNESS

In the store the other day I observed a young mother with an animated toddler in her shopping cart. She had given the child a bag and was handing her lemons to place in it.

"One yellow lemon, two yellow lemons, three yellow lemons," the mother counted as the delighted little girl carefully took each fruit and deposited it in the produce bag. "You're doing a great job of helping Mommy," she continued. "I'm so glad you're my girl!"

The child fairly glowed in the warmth of her mother's love—a love expressed in words both wise and kind. By engaging her daughter in conversation and taking the time to make her feel important, this mother was teaching far more than numbers and colors. She was building a relationship full of love and respect.

Words are so powerful. We can use them to build up or to tear down, to communicate love, indifference, or even hatred. As mothers, aunts, and grandmothers, we have a special opportunity to use our conversations to influence younger people. Not only do they listen to what we say, but they take note of how and when we say it. If they do something clumsy or make a mistake, are we quick to

criticize? Or do we instead use the opportunity to admit our own shortcomings and explain what we have learned from them? Are we as quick to praise a good effort as we are winning results? Do we model conversations that uplift others, or are we primarily occupied with tearing people down? Are we encouragers or discouragers? Speaking from a position of authority is both a privilege and a responsibility.

But what we say is only part of the picture. How we say it is equally important, for the tones of our voices often reveal as much as our words. Which of us cannot recall a time when we listened very carefully to catch our own mother's inflection before deciding how to respond? Was she really angry or merely teasing, testing us, or just curious?

Knowing what to say requires wisdom. Knowing how to say it requires kindness. A woman who submits her heart to God's control learns to do both. Gossip and slander, criticism and nagging, berating, and complaining destroy both family and friends with unwise and unkind words. How much better it is to take the advice of King Lemuel's mother in Proverbs 31:26 and be both wise and kind in all we say.

Prayer: *Father, forgive me for the times I have spoken from selfishness,
not thinking how my words might hurt another.
Help me to submit to You, that I may have the wisdom
to know when to speak and the love to do it with kindness.
Let my words be a reflection of You to my family, friends, and those around me.*

A tender time between mother and child is captured in the painting KNOWLEDGE IS
POWER *by Seymour Joseph Guy. Photo from Christie's Images/Superstock.*

For Mother's Day

Helen Welshimer

Be close, dear God, to that vast throng of women
Whose children still are small—oh, this we pray!
There is so much of hurt and havoc waiting
From which to shield young hearts this Mother's Day.
Help them rear boys and girls, we ask, to follow
The kindly roads, with starry eyes that see
The visions that were meant for youth's awakening.
Let them find signs of new works yet to be!

And God, be with the weary, older mothers,
Who sit alone sometimes and wish they knew
If they have failed because their sons and daughters
Could never scale the heights they wished them to.
Oh, may they know if they have planted wisely
And helped a child stretch tall in heart and mind,
This holds more glory in Thy sight, dear Father,
Than all the hills their children never climbed.

A grandmother shares her love of art and nature with the next generation in this photo by LaFoto/H. Armstrong Roberts.

I can't say for sure just why I started collecting children's books. I like to tell people that building my collection is a practical way of biding my time as I wait for my two grown boys to make me a grandmother. But the books I bring home aren't immediately relegated to the shelf, awaiting those little hands yet to be. More often than not, I find myself sitting down with each new acquisition, curled up in my favorite chair with a cup of tea, immersed in the memories—both of my own faraway childhood and of the less distant days when my two boys were young.

Collecting children's books makes me happy; it is as simple as that. It is not an investment or an obsession, just a pleasant way to spend some of the free time I worked a lifetime to earn. I've met collectors who specialize in one era or another, some who concentrate on one particular author, or a genre, or poetry, prose, or picture books. Some collectors are only interested in books with high monetary value or books they think hold such promise. My method is rather more haphazard, although it can be divided into two categories. I buy new, sturdy editions of my favorite books—books I remember, books I discover while browsing book shops. These line the lower shelves in my living room, just waiting for the next generation of eager, less-than-delicate hands.

The second part of my children's book collection is made up of early editions of the favorites of my own childhood—classics such as the Lassie books, *Charlotte's Web*, and *Black Beauty*—and also the books that my boys loved—*Peter Rabbit*, *Winnie the Pooh*, *Peter Pan*, and anything pertaining to knights, dragons, and castles. These I've earmarked for my grandchildren, too, but not until they are old enough, and gentle enough, to appreciate the treasure that is a good, old book.

One thing I have learned in my years of collecting children's books is that many adults have either forgotten or never truly understood that literature for children is real literature. Just like every other genre, there are forgettable volumes; but there are also true masterpieces. I certainly knew this as a young girl, when I was a devoted and passionate reader; but I may have forgotten it in the years between being a child and being a mother myself.

I recall the very book that reopened my eyes. When my first son was in the midst of his third year and dividing his time between driving me to distraction and melting my heart with his sweetness, a friend gave us a copy of the book *Where the Wild Things Are* by Maurice Sendak. This magically illustrated story of Max and his trip to the Island of the Wild Things has only a handful of words on each page. But those few words worked wonders. They brought me into my child's world, into the vivid life of his imagination, into his struggle to grow up and away from me, while still holding on to my love.

I must have read *Where the Wild Things Are* a thousand times to my young sons over the years, and I never grew tired of it. Although it would be many years before I had the leisure to think of collecting children's books as a hobby, it was with that book, with the insight and enlightenment I found within its pages, that I became a devoted collector.

THE INSIDE STORY

If you would like to collect children's books, here are some interesting facts:

Beloved tales of old are gathered in this photo by Superstock.

HISTORY

• Modern children's literature's earliest roots are folk stories once shared around the family hearth and epic tales told in the halls of kings.

• After the establishment of the printing press in the fifteenth century, many of the great old tales, such as *Fables of Aesop* and *King Arthur*, were printed.

• In the eighteenth century, children's own interests were first considered, and they became the authors' targeted consumers.

• The first children's book published in America was *Spiritual Milk* (1648), which taught Puritan theology along with language skills.

• Until the late 1700s, books were written to instill morals in children. Englishman John Newbery is credited with being the first to recognize the need for playfulness in children's literature.

• Today, an immense range of children's books is available to collectors, who search for (and often pay extra for) first editions, author-inscribed editions, hardback editions, illustrated volumes, like-new volumes, those with dust jackets, or any by well-known authors or illustrators.

FOCUSING A COLLECTION

Many collectors choose to focus on books by a particular author, illustrator, or publisher. Or they may focus on a specific genre. Roughly sixty-nine genres of children's books exist, including:

• Poetry   • Picture books
• ABC books   • Primers
• Adventure stories   • Fairy Tales
• Detective stories   • Pop-up books

ACQUISITION

To begin or add to a collection, the best sources include:
• Reputable dealers
• Antiquarian book sales
• Fellow collectors
• Catalogs of out-of-print books
• Auctions
• Public library book sales
• Antique stores
• Estate sales

CARE

• A cataloging system helps the serious collector keep track of all the books in the collection and their editions and bindings.

• Keep collectible volumes out of direct sunlight and in a room with low humidity and stable temperature.

• Valuable books are best stored in acid-free paper and boxes.

A SLICE OF LIFE

Edgar A. Guest

STORYTELLING

Most every night when they're in bed,
And both their little prayers have said,
They shout for me to come upstairs
And tell them tales of grizzly bears,
And Indians and gypsies bold,
And eagles with the claws that hold
A baby's weight, and fairy sprites
That roam the woods on starry nights.

And I must illustrate these tales,
Must imitate the northern gales
That toss the Indian's canoe,
And show the way he paddles, too.
If in the story comes a bear,
I have to pause and sniff the air
And show the way he climbs the trees
To steal the honey from the bees.

And then I buzz like angry bees
And sting him on his nose and knees
And howl in pain, till Mother cries:
"That pair will never shut their eyes,
While all that noise up there you make;
You're simply keeping them awake."
And then they whisper: "Just one more,"
And once again I'm forced to roar.

New stories every night they ask,
And that is not an easy task;
I have to be so many things,

The frog that croaks, the lark that sings,
The cunning fox, the frightened hen;
　　But just last night they stumped me, when
They wanted me to twist and squirm
　　And imitate an angle worm.

At last they tumble off to sleep,
　　And softly from their room I creep
And brush and comb the shock of hair
　　I tossed about to be a bear.
Then mother says: "Well, I should say
　　You're just as much a child as they."
But you can bet I'll not resign
　　That storytelling job of mine.

Edgar A. Guest began his illustrious career in 1895 at the age of fourteen when his work first appeared in the Detroit Free Press. *His column was syndicated in over three hundred newspapers, and he became known as "The Poet of the People."*

Patrick McRae is an artist who lives in Milwaukee, Wisconsin. He has created nostalgic artwork for Ideals *for more than a decade, and his favorite models are his wife and three children.*

Noseprints

LaVonne Schoneman

Noseprints cover
    my sliding glass door
All in a line—
    one, two, three, four.
My grandchildren left them
    when they came to call;
They stood in a row,
    one, two, three, all
Watching Grandfather hoe
    in the garden nearby
While robins dropped in
    for a worm by and by.
I can't bear to wash it,
    the window, I mean,
Where four little noses
    reflect in the gleam
Of the glass where the sun
    casts its first morning beam.
I look and remember
    my visitors small,
Rejoice in the sunlight,
    and pause to recall
The calling cards left
    on the door by the hall.

Playmates enjoy an afternoon of fun in WINDOW FACES *by Eve DeGrie.*

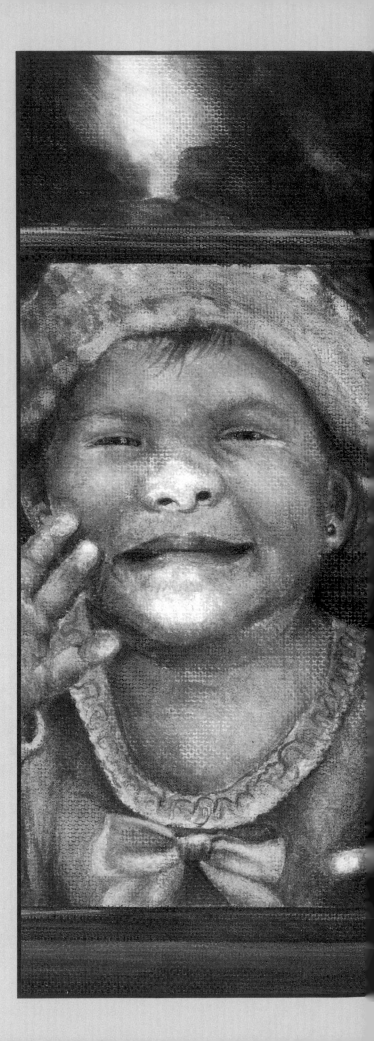

Dream, Dream, Dream

Eugene Field

Dream, dream, dream
  Of meadow, wood, and stream;
Of bird and bee,
  Of flower and tree,
All under the noonday gleam;
  Of the song and play
Of mirthful day—
  Dream, dream, dream!

Dream, dream, dream
  Of glamour, glint, and gleam;
Of the hushaby things
  The night wind sings
To the moon and the stars abeam;
  Of whimsical sights
In the land o' sprites
  Dream, dream, dream!

In Donald Zolan's painting CAT NAP, *a favorite kitty knows
there is no better place for a nap than in a little girl's arms.*

Motherhood

Katherine Edelman

I love to watch a mother's face
  As she bends low above a crib,
Smoothing with gentle, easy touch
  A careless curl or wrinkled bib.

It seems an angel's tenderness
  In every gentle movement lies,
And that a bit of heaven itself
  Is mirrored in her shining eyes.

And as I watch, my thoughts go far,
  To Nazareth, that hallowed town,
And fancy brings before my eyes
  A mother in a blue-gold gown.

I see her bend above a Babe—
  A Child that came from heaven above—
I see her stroke a dimpled hand
  And whisper words of tender love.

I love to watch a mother's face,
  For every mother seems to bear
Some small resemblance to that one
  That gave Him such devoted care.

Lullabies

Starrlette L. Howard

I've yet to meet the angels
That are in heaven's place,
But I've seen the glow of motherhood
And a fragile baby's face.
I'm sure there's more to measure
Than only gold could bring,
And I'm sure all heaven listens
To a mother when she sings.

Cherished mementos of a new addition to the family are displayed in this image by Diane Padys/FPG International.

EUGENE FIELD

The work of Eugene Field is familiar to anyone who has had the pleasure of reading poetry to children. The sweet and sad "Little Boy Blue," the amusing poem "The Gingham Cat and the Calico Dog," and the endearing lullaby "Wynken, Blynken, and Nod" are only three of the more famous of a large body of work. Look in any collection of poems for the young, and something by Eugene Field is likely to be included.

But Field himself never hoped to be remembered for his children's verse. Near the end of his life, assessing his career and reputation, Field despaired that he had become known as "the poet of childhood." A journalist for two decades, Field believed his poetry unfairly overshadowed his more serious work as a newspaper columnist. As with every writer, it was for the public to decide which was his most important contribution. Field's daily column for the Chicago *Morning News* was widely read and admired; yet the public chose to think of him not as a newspaper columnist, but as the man who wrote "Little Boy Blue."

Eugene Field was born in St. Louis in 1850 to Roswell and Frances Field. Roswell Field was a Saint Louis attorney who gained national prominence for years of service as a lawyer for Dred Scott in the famous slave trials. Eugene Field's early years were happy ones, spent enjoying the close company of his father and brother and the neighborhood children. But when he was only six, his mother died; and he and his brother were sent to live with relatives in the rural town of Amherst, Massachusetts. Field lived there happily until 1868 when he enrolled at Williams College. He went on to try two more universities before he abandoned his education short of a degree to marry and begin a career. Field chose journalism and set about earning the living he needed to support his wife, Julia, and their family, which would grow to include eight children.

Field held a string of newspaper jobs until 1883 when he joined the *Morning News* as a daily columnist. At the time, personal opinion columns were unusual, and Field became somewhat of a pioneer in the genre. Writing under the title "Sharps and Flats," he drew a large readership with an assortment of writing—satires, literary notes, humorous verse, children's poems, stories from his childhood, and reflections on family, politics, and society in nineteenth-century Chicago. Field's personality shone through in his work; his wit, his charm, his love of the practical joke, and his affection for his growing brood of children all worked to earn him the title of "father of the personal byline column." He went on to publish several collections of his writings and became somewhat of a midwestern celebrity and a sought-after public speaker.

In 1895, at the peak of his career, Eugene Field died. He was only forty-five years old when he wrote his last column, and his career was cut short before he reached what likely would have been his most productive age. As the years passed after his death, his reputation as a journalist gradually faded. But his children's poetry—the writing that he considered less valuable and less interesting than his more "serious" body of work—never fell out of favor. The nickname he had gained in his own lifetime, the nickname he never embraced, stuck. Eugene Field was remembered as the "poet of childhood."

In the introduction to a posthumously published collection of Eugene Field's verse, his brother Roswell Field, Jr. describes their shared, happy childhood. He recalls that his brother was neither a particularly distinguished student nor a boy of great seriousness. Instead, he was a child with a boisterous sense of humor, a quick wit, a knack for rhyming, and an expansive love for animals. Roswell describes how his brother always cared for a wide variety of animals and was known for taking in strays. He would bestow each creature not only with a distinctive and colorful nickname but also with a unique voice and character. Roswell also recalls that Eugene would often celebrate his animals by creating impromptu verse about them.

The picture of young Eugene Field that emerges from his brother's fond reminiscing is one of a boy who embraced the joys of childhood. It is easy to project forward to a man who understood children well because he remembered vividly what it was to be young. Perhaps, had he lived longer, Field would have come to embrace his reputation as a writer for children and would have come to see what his brother, and his readers, saw so well: Eugene Field was a man with a special gift, a man who shared that gift with the world through his delightful poems of childhood.

Nancy Skarmeas is a book editor and mother of a toddler, Gordon, who keeps her and her husband quite busy at their home in New Hampshire. Her Greek and Irish ancestry has fostered a lifelong interest in research and history.

THE EUGENE FIELD HOUSE
ST. LOUIS, MISSOURI

Michelle Prater Burke

Many authors and poets attribute their inspiration to their childhood years, the time they spent with family, and the memories that built their past. Knowing this, I was not surprised to discover the type of home enjoyed by the young Eugene Field. Field's future reputation as the poet laureate of children was assured years before he ever put pen to paper. It began in a home full of love and community in St. Louis, Missouri.

In 1829, two decades before Eugene Field's birth, one of the founders of St. Louis, Auguste Chouteau, died, and his land was deeded to the city of St. Louis. Sixteen years later, in 1845, with St. Louis still clustered close to the Mississippi River and its steamboat commerce, a man named Edward Walsh leased the land and built a twelve-unit row house known as Walsh's Row.

Attorney Roswell Martin Field and his wife, Frances, leased the second unit from the south end of Walsh's Row in 1850. The three-story home had classic Federal-style architecture with a recessed Greek Revival entryway. The Fields' first child, Eugene, was born at their new home on September 3, 1850. The boy's early life was a happy one, for he shared a close relationship with both his younger brother and his father. Roswell Field enjoyed being around children and loved to sit on the front steps of the house in the evenings and play the violin, beckoning the neighborhood children to gather around. After the death of Frances Field in 1856, Roswell Field sent Eugene and his younger brother to school in Massachusetts, in part to distance his sons from the Civil War disturbances taking place in Missouri. But the children eagerly returned to the house in Walsh's Row each summer, and it remained the family home until 1864.

Eugene Field always held a dear spot in his heart for his childhood home and the evenings he had spent surrounded by family and young friends. When he visited the house as an adult, he took the doorbell and newel-post with him as he left (even though the house was occupied by another family at the time). In 1902, seven years after Field's death, Mark Twain dedicated a plaque that can still be seen on the front of the house. It reads, "Here was born Eugene Field, the poet, 1850–1895."

In 1934, Walsh's Row was scheduled for demolition when Irving Dilliard, editor of the *St. Louis Post-Dispatch*, wrote a spirited editorial decrying the destruction of Eugene Field's birthplace, and a committee was formed to preserve the home. The following year, schoolchildren in the St. Louis Public Schools saved their pennies and contributed nearly two thousand dollars to restore the home of their beloved poet, and it opened as a museum in December of 1936.

The Eugene Field House was the first historic house museum in Missouri to open to the public on a regular basis and is now the oldest remaining residence in downtown St. Louis. Its rooms are also home to the St. Louis Toy Museum and its wonderful toy collection with pieces that date from 1800 to the present. Visitors can enjoy an 1837 dollhouse, complete with its original furnishings, that was once owned by a young girl in Philadelphia; a French tricycle made in 1860 that is shaped like a horse, pedaled by hand, and guided by foot; an 1857 rocking horse; and numerous antique dolls, which were Eugene Field's favorite toys.

In one of his poems, Field wrote, "Up in the attic where I slept / When I was a boy, a little boy, / In through the lattice the moonlight crept, / Bringing a tide of dreams that swept." It was this sort of memory of the house and its first family that inspired the works of this well-loved poet, and I have no doubt that Eugene Field would approve of how the rooms of his former home continue to hold pleasant reminders of childhood long ago.

Eugene Field's desk remains at his home in St. Louis. Photo by Jack Zehrt.

MY DAUGHTER

Jan Jones

Soon enough my daughter will know
that this world is not all butterflies and caterpillars,
   long walks near pebbled streams,
   picnics and teeter-totters,
   blowing bubbles on breezy days,
   loving hugs and squeezes,
   sweet lullabies and good-night kisses.

But for this moment, this precious moment, let me
drink in and enjoy her giggles and laughter,
   ruffles and bows,
   rocking-horse bounces,
   birthdays with playmates,
   sweetness and innocence.

And may these memories linger
and help us both through the difficult years
   which bridge childhood to adulthood,
   where we will bond again,
   this time, as friends.

RIDDLE

Oneita G. Fisher

I try to guess the things
My children will remember:
   The playhouse where
   A mouse filed claim,
   The funny hat I wore but once,
   The way we like our table set beneath
   The window where the blue jays flash,
   Trails the lambs made in the lane,
   The wide back steps
   Where raindrops splash.
Such fragments dot the plain of childhood
And become as jewels for future counting,
Hoarded in the mind.
These treasures I would see and polish well;
But they are not for me to find.

A family enjoys lunch under the trees in NOON *by Plinio Nomellini.*
Photo from Private Collection /Fratelli Alinari/Superstock.

JOURNEY

Margaret H. Hasbargen

Your small hand still clings tightly to my own
Along dark halls to hush your little fears;
Yet you will cross this darkened hall alone,
Unfearing, in the span of a few years.
You come to me still with your woe and joy
(My heart is humbled by your trusting eyes),
And I am glad you're still a little boy
Who thinks that I am kind and strong and wise.

And when your small hand clings to mine no more,
May you have found some worthy work to do.
And may your eager heart behold a score
Of dreams; may love and courage see you through
Upon the journey you have just begun.
My heart enfolds this prayer for you, my son.

*The best gifts a mother can give her
child are roots and wings.*

—Chinese proverb

A young boy sets out on the day's journey.
Photo by Superstock.

Bits & Pieces

Tired nature's sweet restorer, balmy sleep!
—EDWARD YOUNG

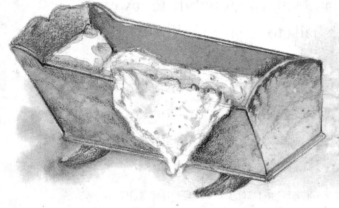

Rock-a-bye baby, on the tree top,
When the wind blows, the cradle will rock;
When the bough breaks, the cradle will fall;
Down will come baby, cradle and all.
—ENGLISH NURSERY RHYME

I will both lay me down in peace,
and sleep: for thou, LORD, only
makest me dwell in safety.
—PSALM 4:8

To all, to each, a fair good-night,
And pleasing dreams,
and slumbers light.
—SIR WALTER SCOTT

Father in heaven, when the thought of You wakes in our hearts, let it not awaken like a frightened bird flying about in dismay, but like a child waking from its sleep with a heavenly smile.
—SØREN KIERKEGAARD

The day is done, and the darkness
Falls from the wings of night,
As a feather is wafted downward
From an eagle in his flight.
—HENRY WADSWORTH LONGFELLOW

O sleep, O gentle sleep,
Nature's soft nurse!
—WILLIAM SHAKESPEARE

Hush, my dear, lie still and slumber!
Holy angels guard thy bed!
Heavenly blessings without number
Gently falling on thy head.
—ISAAC WATTS

Sleep is God's celestial nurse who croons
away our consciousness.
—OSWALD CHAMBERS

O bed! O bed! Delicious bed!
That heaven upon earth to the
weary head.
—THOMAS HOOD

Tribute

Isla Paschal Richardson

A mother's love! Unselfishness it breathes,
And constancy and purity. Akin
To love divine it changeless glows, steadfast,
Unfaltering, true, the mother-heart within.

A mother's care! The countless hours, the years
Of watchfulness, can children understand?
The child sees flower-grown paths, not dreams of stones
Removed. His guard, her eyes; his guide, her hand.

A mother's hopes! How hard we'd strive to make
Those dreams and hopes that fill her heart come true,
The shining goal that she has set for us
All through the years—if we as children knew!

A mother's prayers! They lift her spirit up.
Who knows the blessings that they bring, the fears
Her faith has overcome? Always her prayers
Follow her child, are with him through the years.

I cannot tell you how I love you, dear,
But with my baby in my arms, I pray
That God may help me be a mother true
As you have been and are to me today.

The pink beauties of a springtime garden are
pictured in this photo by Nancy Matthews.

Remember When

From *Washday at Dawn*

Marjorie Holmes

The modern ease and convenience of our automated lives have taken something besides drudgery out of the domestic scene. Many tender side benefits and compensations, peculiarly female. For one thing, women have been robbed of the unspoken Monday morning competition that used to exist, at least in most small towns.

The truly ambitious housewife would struggle out of bed before daylight in the fervent hope of being the first to have her clothes on the line. Oh, those flapping banners, proudly proclaiming a woman's zeal! In our neighborhood everybody finally gave up trying to beat Mrs. Mansky, whose lines were always snapping and taunting their triumph by dawn. But the others—those who valued their standing at least—got in there and fought it out to be second. True, there were a few sluggards (my mother, for one) who refused to compete, and sometimes didn't have the evidence of their efforts out till after ten, or sometimes noon. Who sometimes even—imagine!—chose to wash on another *day*. But such rugged individuals were the exception.

The only times Mrs. Mansky didn't win the contest were when she was away visiting her daughter in Cherokee, or too sick to stagger forth with the bulging baskets at all. Everybody was so programmed to starting the week with Mrs. Mansky's washing

Neighbors pause from their workday to share the latest gossip.
Photo by Grant Heilman Photography.

that when her lines were vacant there was an uneasiness in the air. And although some women gloated, privately they were distressed. Once, when she was in the hospital six weeks with a broken hip, they couldn't stand it; they took turns going to her house and doing her wash. What's more, they saw to it that the Monday morning sunrise continued to do honor to her good name.

The whiteness of the clothes was another status symbol. No hucksters were needed to rouse our mothers with a feverish pitch about "ring around the collar" and "tattle-tale gray." They were in there pitching themselves, with strong yellow soap shaved into a scalding wash boiler, and a scrub board on which to bloody the knuckles if necessary to be sure that the dishtowels and the shirts and the long winter woolens came clean. . . .

Mother cheerfully resisted joining the race to the line. "Let them break their necks if they want to, I'll get mine out when I good and please." But she more than compensated by the pride she took in the ultimate display. "It's funny," she would mumble around the wooden pins in her mouth, "but I really *like* to hang out the clothes!" And no artist arranging his paintings did so with more care than that with which she riveted her products to the line. Sheets neatly doubled, bottoms up so that the breeze could blow

Wearing bonnets to shield them from the spring sun, a family shares the washday chores. Photo by Grant Heilman Photography.

them dry. And no helter-skelter arrangements either: all sheets marching together, all pillowcases on parade, then the rest of the aristocratic whites, which got priority in the water. After that the coloreds, each carefully with his kind, so that the rows of shirts or dresses dancing were like a chain of paper dolls.

She even made sure the colors didn't clash—no reds next to pinks—and entertained herself by hanging harmonious shades side by side.

"Slovenly" she dubbed anyone who bunched things carelessly together or tossed them pinless on a line. And rags or worn unmentionables were discreetly dried inside. "A woman is judged by her washing," she declared. And she was right. For people walked more then and had time to study not only your curtains and your flower beds but your clotheslines as they strolled by.

Sometimes, at our imploring, she reversed the sheets so that we might dive and fumble between their damply flapping sides. Or, washing and airing blankets, she would help us peg them into the ground for tents. We would creep in on all fours and sometimes camp all day, setting up housekeeping with tea sets and dolls and limp bouquets of dandelions. How secret and snug it was, hot and fragrant with sun and grassy earth. While outside you could hear the sheets and towels snapping as your mother visited with a neighbor across the fence.

It was fun to help take the dry things down; they collapsed with such sweetness against your face to be folded and tucked into the creaking basket. The whites were sometimes so dazzling they hurt the eyes. . . .

Hard labor though the laundry was, a woman was repaid by her sense of personal value. With loving hands and arms and back she kept her family clean. Her clotheslines were her banner, proudly flown.

A MASQUERADE

Author Unknown

A little old woman before me
Went slowly down the street;
Walking as if aweary
Were her feeble, tottering feet.

From under her old poke bonnet
I caught a gleam of snow,
And her waving cap string floated,
Like a pennon, to and fro.

In the folds of her rusty mantle,
Sudden her footstep caught,
And I sprang to keep her from falling,
With a touch as quick as thought.

When under the old poke bonnet
I saw a winsome face,
Framed in with the flaxen ringlets
Of my wee daughter Grace.

Mantle and cap together
Dropped off at my very feet;
And there stood the little fairy,
Beautiful, blushing, sweet!

Will it be like this, I wonder,
When at last we come to stand
On the golden, ringing pavement
Of the blessed, blessed land?

Losing the rusty garments
We wore in the years of time,
Will our better selves spring backward,
Serene in a youth sublime?

Instead of the shapes that hid us,
And made us old and gray,
Shall we get our child-hearts back again,
With a brightness that will stay?

I thought—but my little daughter
Slipped her dimpled hand in mine;
"I was only playing," she whispered,
"That I was ninety-nine."

A day spent playing in Mother's closet is a happy memory for child-hood friends. Photo by Telegraph Colour Library/FPG International.

A Mother's Way

Marga Joerden

I know the other paths you might have chosen;
But your heart, to duty born, must still be true.
Your own desires, your wishes for the future,
Were all abandoned while you saw me through.
I made you smile sometimes, and caused you heartache;
You spent your life unstintingly to raise
Me to adulthood, strong in faith, inspired
By your dedication through those painful days.
On summer nights we walked and sang our songs
Beneath the brilliant Arizona stars,
Explored moon-misted visions, cried our hearts out
For hurt and beauty both; those years were ours.
I freely dipped my cup into your pool
Of choices, raising it, filled to the brim,
To sip of courage, duty, and devotion,
Forsaking lesser loves for love of Him.
When life is dealing out its hurtful lessons,
And I must choose the better thing to do,
I'm so grateful that I've had you as my model,
That God gave me a mother such as you.

Grandmother's treasures remind us of yesteryear.
Photo by Dianne Dietrich Leis.

THROUGH MY WINDOW
Pamela Kennedy

Art by Pat Thompson

MOM.COM, SUBJ: FRESHMAN YEAR

Sept. 10—Dear Mom, college is great! My roommate is pretty cool and the guys next door have an awesome CD collection. There's a get-acquainted dance in the main lounge Friday night. Why did you buy that huge bottle of vitamins? Don't you think I know how to take care of myself? Yes, the clothes I brought are fine. I told you everyone wears German sandals. When it gets cold you just put on wool socks with them. Don't worry so much. I'll be fine!

Oct. 8—Dear Mom, My roommate has been sleeping through most of his morning classes. He's up all night with the rockers next door. I really like my biology professor. He knows so much

about everything. I may want to major in environmental science. Did you know that one of the main reasons the rain forests in Brazil are disappearing is because of beef cattle? I need some new underwear. Mine is all pink after I accidentally got my red sweatshirt mixed in with the white stuff. And could you send some wool socks? It's freezing! Got to get to the library.

Nov. 2—Thanks for the socks and underwear, but next time you send cookies don't write "Goodie Express" on the box. The guys said they were great. I met this guy Jeff who is going to be stuck here over the holiday, and I wondered if he could come home with me for Thanksgiving. He's a vegan, so you might want to think about something other than turkey for dinner. No, I don't need an iron. Mark showed me this neat trick where you just toss a damp washcloth in the dryer with your shirt for a few minutes and it takes out most of the wrinkles. Of course I know beef cattle don't eat trees, Mom. The farmers cut the trees to plant grass.

Nov. 15—Dear Mom, No, a vegan is not someone from Las Vegas. It's someone who doesn't eat anything that comes from animals. Thanks for letting Jeff come for Thanksgiving. I know he likes tofu and organically grown things, so anything like that would be fine. We'll see you soon.

Dec. 3—Hi Mom, I'm running a little low on cash, but have been selling the vitamins. Everyone seems to have a cold. If you want an idea for me for Christmas, I could use some warm boots. I've decided to quit eating beef. If I don't take a stand on this, my grandchildren may never even see a rain forest. Hey, marking the box of cookies as "Medical Supplies" was a stroke of genius. Thanks.

Jan. 6—Dear Mom, It was so great being home for Christmas. Thanks for the boots and the other stuff. Did I tell you my roommate flunked out? It's kind of quiet here without him, even though he slept most of the time. Did I tell you Jeff is picketing the dining hall because they don't serve tofu lasagna?

Jan. 22—Dear Mom, What's good for a sore throat? It is freezing here and my professors are really piling on the work. I don't know if I want to major in environmental science anymore. Nothing sounds really exciting right now. I think I'll go to bed.

Feb. 12—Dear Mom, Thanks for the care package. The herbal tea helped, and the macaroni and cheese was easy to fix on the hot plate. I didn't have a strainer for the pasta, so I poked some holes in an old frisbee and it worked great! I got this new roommate who sits at his computer all the time. I'm not sure what he's doing. A bunch of us are going to try snowboarding at the mountain this weekend.

March 5—Dear Mom, Now that my sprained ankle is better, it's easier getting to and from classes. Did I tell you about Keri, a girl who lives in the dorm next to mine? She was really nice and helped me get some of the assignments I missed when I was in the infirmary. We've been doing lots of studying together. You'd like her. Do you believe in love at first sight?

March 10—Dear Mom, A bunch of us are going to Ben's cabin at Birch Island for the first part of spring break. I'll still be able to get home for three days. We're going to fish and get clams and oysters and sort of live off the land—a manly time!

April 5—Dear Mom, I really appreciated the way you let everyone crash at the house for spring break. I guess Ben hadn't been to the cabin in a long time and didn't realize the power was off and the roof was missing in spots. Sorry about all the dirty laundry, but after the rainstorm things got pretty muddy. Can you believe only one more quarter to go?

April 20—Dear Mom, My computer geek roomie just got put on academic probation. He was trying to attend class via the internet or something. Did I tell you I'm really enjoying my humanities class? Did you know that Einstein had this whole theory about time and how you could transcend it by going faster than the speed of light? I may want to major in philosophy. Keri loves to discuss ideas. I think we're really compatible. Gotta run, I'm late.

May 15—Dear Mom, I can't believe my first year at college is almost over. I really feel I've matured a lot being away from home and having to think for myself and make my own decisions. I'm much more independent. My last final is on June 4. Could you send a plane ticket for that afternoon? Do you know any place that sells beef that's not from Brazil? I'm dying for a steak dinner. See you soon.

Pamela Kennedy is a freelance writer of short stories, articles, essays, and children's books. Wife of a retired naval officer and mother of three children, she has made her home on both U.S. coasts and currently resides in Honolulu, Hawaii.

To My Daughter
at Her Wedding

Grace V. Watkins

He slips the golden circle on your finger,
And in your eyes a wonder-lighted smile
Shines through the luster of the dreams that linger,
Still as the burning candles by the aisle.
Oh, wear love proudly—it is a precious thing,
Woven of diamond joy and pearl-white pain,
Brighter than meadows where the bluebirds sing,
Lovelier than a field in summer rain.
And if you walk the uplands on a highway
Lighted with joy as golden as the sun,
Or some day travel down a shadowed byway
Alone, remember, child, all paths are one.
Beyond the clouds above the highest hill,
Through dawn or dusk the stars are shining still.

To My Husband
at Our Daughter's Wedding

Grace V. Watkins

Within this quiet rose-and-candle hour,
You touch my hand and swiftly, silently,
I am the bride, as slender as a flower;
You are the groom, with all the years to be
A garden in our hearts, a gladness stirred
To glory past the scope of song or word.

Perhaps they will have rugged hills to climb,
But if they find the deep abundant streams
Of healing faith along the roads of time,
No cloud can ever dim their shining dreams;
And oh, the journeying will be more bright
Than any universe of golden light!

*Delicate roses remain as souvenirs of a glorious
wedding day. Photo by Nancy Matthews.*

Family Recipes

What better time to wed than in the springtime, when the earth seems to celebrate along with you. The following recipes offer scrumptious fare for the next bridal shower you attend. Be sure to pass a copy of each recipe along to the new bride! We would love to try your best-loved recipe too. Mail a typed copy of the recipe along with your name, address, and phone number to Ideals Magazine, ATTN: Recipes, P.O. Box 305300, Nashville, Tennessee 37230. We will pay $10 for each recipe used.

Maids of Honor
Feryl E. Harris of Pennsboro, West Virginia

2 cups all-purpose flour
1 teaspoon salt
⅔ cup plus 1 tablespoon shortening
3 to 4 tablespoons water
    Raspberry jam
1 box white cake mix

2 cups powdered sugar
1 teaspoon vanilla
2 tablespoons butter
1 to 2 tablespoons milk
    Maraschino cherries

In a large bowl, sift together flour and salt. Using a pastry blender, cut in shortening until mixture resembles coarse crumbs. Add water, a tablespoon at a time, mixing each moistened section with a fork. Form dough into a ball and roll out small portions at a time to a ⅛-inch thickness. With a biscuit cutter that is four inches in diameter, cut out 24 circles of dough. Press dough circles into ungreased cupcake pans (the dough should be even with the top of the pan). Spoon 1 generous teaspoon raspberry jam into each circle. Set aside.

Preheat oven to 375° F. Prepare cake mix according to package directions. Divide mix among dough circles, filling each ¾ full. Bake 18 to 20 minutes or until toothpick inserted in the center of each cupcake comes out clean. Place pan on wire rack to cool.

In a small bowl, combine powdered sugar and vanilla. Using a pastry blender, cut in butter until mixture resembles coarse crumbs. Add enough milk to moisten and mix until smooth. Spread frosting over each cupcake. Break cherries in half and place one half atop each cupcake. Makes 2 dozen cupcakes.

Hawaiian Wedding Cake
Eleanor L. Baker of Ridgeley, West Virginia

1 box yellow cake mix
1 3½-ounce box vanilla instant pudding mix
1 8-ounce package cream cheese, softened
2 cups milk

1 20-ounce can crushed pineapple, drained well
1 9-ounce carton whipped topping
½ cup chopped walnuts
¼ cup coconut

Prepare and bake cake mix according to package directions in two 9-inch cake pans. Cool. In a large bowl, whip together pudding mix, cream cheese, and milk. Let set 5 minutes, then spread between layers and over cake. Spread pineapple over cake. Cover with whipped topping. Sprinkle with nuts and coconut. Refrigerate until serving. Makes one cake.

Aunt Fannie's Tea Cakes

Jeannine Long of Lebanon, Tennessee

½ cup butter, softened
¾ cup granulated sugar
½ teaspoon salt
1 teaspoon vanilla extract

½ teaspoon lemon extract
2 eggs
2 cups all-purpose flour

In a large bowl, cream butter with sugar until light and fluffy. Stir in salt and flavorings. Add eggs one at a time, mixing well after each addition. Slowly add flour, mixing well. Cover dough with plastic wrap and chill 1 hour.

Preheat oven to 400° F. Divide dough in half. On a lightly floured board, roll out one half of dough until approximately ¼-inch thick. Using a biscuit cutter, cut out rounds of dough and place on an ungreased cookie sheet. Repeat with remaining dough. Bake 10 to 12 minutes or until lightly browned. Makes 24 tea cakes.

Wedding Cookies

Alma R. Toth of Springfield, Ohio

1 cup butter, softened
½ cup powdered sugar
1 teaspoon vanilla
2¼ cups all-purpose flour

¼ teaspoon salt
¾ cup finely chopped nuts
Additional powdered sugar

Preheat oven to 400° F. In a large bowl, cream butter until light and fluffy. Slowly beat in powdered sugar and vanilla, mixing well. Stir in flour and salt; mix well. Fold in nuts. Shape dough into 1-inch balls and place on an ungreased cookie sheet. Bake 8 to 11 minutes or until cookies are set but not brown. While cookies are still warm, roll in powdered sugar. Place on wire rack to cool. When cool, roll in sugar again. Makes 4 dozen cookies.

Fruit Slush

Mrs. Pauline McGinnis of Altoona, Pennsylvania

2 11-ounce cans mandarin orange segments, drained
1 20-ounce can crushed pineapple in pineapple juice
1½ cups water

1 6-ounce can frozen orange juice concentrate, thawed
1 6-ounce jar maraschino cherries with juice
3 medium ripe bananas, sliced

In a large bowl, combine all ingredients and mix well. Spoon approximately ½ cup of mixture into an 8-ounce freezer-safe cup. Repeat for remaining cups. Cover each with plastic wrap; place in freezer at least four hours. Before serving, let stand at room temperature 30 to 60 minutes. Individual cups may be thawed in the microwave on high for 1 to 1½ minutes. Makes 15 servings.

RAIN AT NIGHT

Isla Paschal Richardson

Whenever it starts raining in the night,

I wake and, sleepily, without a light,

Grope mentally around the house outdoors

For some forgotten plaything, on which pours

A steady shower where busy feet played late;

Tired little feet, forsaking doll and skate,

A red tricycle or a shoe-box train.

How often I've retrieved them in the rain!

And then, remembering, I lie back down.

The one who owned those toys lives across town,

And now is tiptoeing to her door, no doubt,

In search of truant toys and, reaching out,

Brings in an armored tank or battered jeep

Belonging to her son—aged five—asleep.

A late-spring garden holds remainders from a day at play among the blossoms. Photo by Gay Bumgarner.

Grandma's Quilt

E. K. Alaskey

She started the quilt when just a girl
And added to it through the years,
Each patch compiled of memories
Connected by past smiles and tears.

A piece of cloth from a party dress
She wore to her very first dance;
A little square of bright red plaid,
Memento of a past romance.

A swatch of lace from her wedding dress;
Flannel saved from a baby shawl;
A bit of a boy's worn blue pants,
When he grew from short to tall.

Patch after patch, a tale unfolds,
Sewn with Grandma's love and care,
Her life recorded in the quilt,
In each and every cherished square.

Cradle Quilt

June Masters Bacher

The quilt that cradled you
As sweetly you slept,
Did you trace its pattern
Of memories kept?
Captured in abstract
Circle and square
To cross-stitch distance
From here to there:
A block of black velvet
From Granny's chair;
A first-day-of-school skirt;
Locks of your hair;
An ivory petticoat's clinging caress;
A taffeta whisper of wedding dress—
Cloth, binding a patchwork
Of shapeless things,
Created from chaos,
And given wings.

A family's history has been stitched into this colorful Ohio-star quilt. Photo by Superstock.

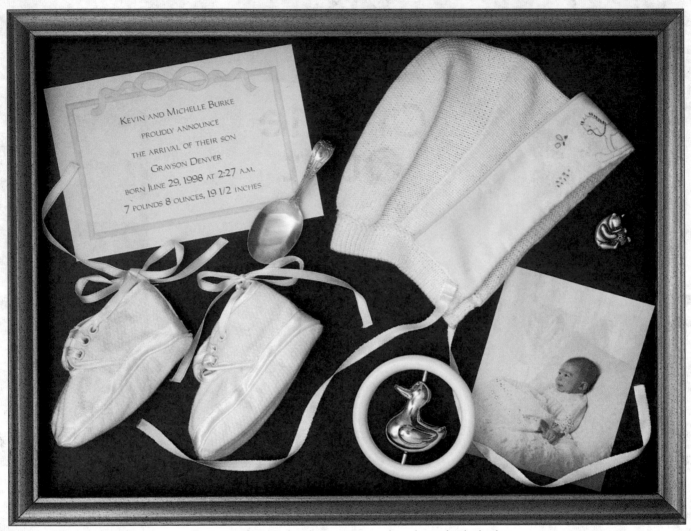

KEVIN AND MICHELLE BURKE
PROUDLY ANNOUNCE
THE ARRIVAL OF THEIR SON
GRAYSON DENVER
BORN JUNE 29, 1998 AT 2:27 A.M.
7 POUNDS 8 OUNCES, 19 1/2 INCHES

Memories of a son's first days are preserved in a keepsake shadowbox.

SHADOWBOX

Michelle Prater Burke

I have always been one of those organized perfectionists who appreciates a good plan and a good list. I have even been known to add completed tasks to my to-do list just so I can immediately mark them off. From my day-to-day activities to my life's goals, organization and forethought have kept me grounded. So when my husband and I discovered we were expecting our first child, I set out to spend my pregnancy planning and producing the perfect setting in which to bring my perfect child.

In my first-trimester good humors, I touted plans to organize my entire house, design a story-book nursery, and handsew a keepsake layette, all before my July due date. I would chronicle every moment of my pregnancy and my child's first years of life in an archival-quality scrapbook, filling it with my reflections, mementos, and words of wisdom.

Eight months later, as I stared in awe at my tiny newborn son, I wondered where the time had gone. Somewhere between the bouts of morning sickness and the weekend my husband and I spent trying to correctly assemble a crib, my grand plans had been lost. But surprisingly, the sense of accomplishment I once felt after completing a project paled when compared to the joy of watching my son discover his toes for the first time. It was my first lesson in parenting—life is no longer predictable.

But although I had no time for detailed scrapbook projects, I was still wishing I could somehow preserve some of the mementos from those precious first days. Then one afternoon an image in a catalog caught my eye. The picture was of a shadowbox framing several antique baby items. My mind immediately began thinking of all of my son's collectibles. What a simple and classic way to preserve my memories!

Shadowboxes have long served as ideal display cases for treasures, whether valuable or not. The boxes' popularity is attributed to the late American artist Joseph Cornell. In the 1930s and 1940s, Cornell, who has been called the master of the shadowbox, became known for creating "memory boxes" full of seemingly disparate items grouped according to the associations they evoked. Others soon realized that even modest household knick-knacks become artistic compositions when brought together and presented creatively.

The possibilities for creating a keepsake shadowbox are endless. A child's box could include a lock of hair, a favorite toy, or his or her first drawing. A collection honoring a grandmother might contain a lace handkerchief, a strand of pearls, a beloved locket. Or the box could preserve a wedding day by framing the invitation, dried flowers, and sheet music to the couple's first dance. Any mementos, from a sampling of fishing lures to a collection of thimbles, can be displayed in a shadowbox and given instant heirloom status.

To create a shadowbox for my son, I purchased a ready-made one at a crafts store. However, any frame shop could construct a box to your size and depth specifications. For a more casual look, you could use old drawers or crates and display them without glass. The back and interior walls of a shadowbox can be covered with any fabric or paper. (It is easiest to cut pieces of cardboard to size, cover them with fabric, then glue the pieces into the box.) Velvet is a popular choice for lining the box; but for a unique backdrop, consider wallpaper, maps, giftwrap, old letters, or any lining that complements the box's theme. Once you've chosen and arranged the items you would like to frame, you can attach them to the back of the box using heavy-duty, double-sided mounting tape. Another choice is to sew the items onto foam board or mount them with small pins.

I lined my shadowbox with deep blue paper to match my son's nursery and used mounting tape to carefully secure the items inside. His birth announcement and silver rattle were my first choices; then I added his silver spoon, an embroidered bonnet, his first booties, and a photograph of him wearing his great-grandfather's antique gown. The result was a beautiful and permanent collage of memories, completed in very little time.

My son is now six months old, and I realize that the days of planning my schedule down to the minute are long past, forgotten among the diaper changes and midnight feedings. I've learned to relax my expectations and cherish each moment with my child; the few lists I do make include plans for play groups instead of dinner parties. I hope one day my son will look at the items displayed in his shadowbox and be assured of how much I treasure him and every grin he offers throughout our unpredictable day.

MOTHER'S DAY

Author Unknown

It's a long, long time and a weary way
From the hills of youth and the yesterday,
From the bending trees and the games we played,
And the bubbling stream where we used to wade,
And the old rope swing, and the blue above,
And the father's laugh and the mother's love.

It's a long, long way and the dust lies deep
On the winding road, and we're nearing sleep;
But ever and ever we look back there
Where the woods are green and the skies are fair,
And the old rope swing and the glad days are,
And we grieve and wish it were not so far.

We wish indeed it were not so far
To the curving stream and the sandy bar,
And the stones where the grayfish lurked and hid,
And the shallow stretch where the water slid
Like a lace-edged curtain, and cattails stood—
It were not so far to the wind-stirred wood.

But it is, it is far to the yesterday,
And the tracks in the dust all point one way.
From youth they come down the winding track,
And never a footprint wanders back
To the blossomed ways where the songs were sung
That we can't forget, when the world was young.

To the mother love and the father squeeze,
And the purple nights and the waiting knees
Where we perched and harked to the twice-told tales,
And our eyes grew round; and oh, the jeweled sails
Of fancy only can waft us back
Down the stream of time to the youth we lack.

So we're wearing a lovely rose today
To the mother love of the yesterday,
And the father—loving—above our heart,
And our eyes dim with the tears that start
Unbidden—and years in the future—thus
Shall our children wear a rose for us.

A springtime scene in the country is portrayed in Jane Wooster Scott's painting MOTHER'S DAY. *Collection of Mr. and Mrs. Granville Van Dusen/Superstock.*

Lilac Time

Jessie Wilmore Murton

Let me go home when it is lilac time!
When purple fragrance drifts
    through warm spring rain
As liquid and as silver as the chime
Of crystal bells; or sunlight, like a stain
From heaven's bright tip-tilted bowl of blue,
Spills goldenly on shimmering heart-shaped leaves;
While wayward tendrils cling, unguided, to
The edges of old shingles and brown eaves
That once had sheltered me.

The sagging door
Will faintly creak at lifting of the latch,
And soft light streams across the dusty floor,
To tremble lightly where the rainbows catch
In silken webs. . . . Then, on my heart, some past
Strange quietness, a something closely kin
To peace that once I knew, shall fall at last,
When, with the closing of the door, the din
Of years is shut without.

And memory's chime
Will drift like subtle fragrance through bright rain,
Or cling as wayward tendrils, when they climb
Unguided over scars of former pain.
Let me go home—when it is lilac time!

Lilacs cover a rustic fence in Martha's Vineyard, Massachusetts.
Photo by Dianne Dietrich Leis.

OUR HERITAGE

TO MY DEAR AND LOVING HUSBAND

Anne Bradstreet

If ever two were one, then surely we.

   If ever man were lov'd by wife, then thee;

If ever wife were happy in a man,

   Compare with me ye women if you can.

I prize thy love more than whole mines of gold,

   Or all the riches that the east doth hold.

My love is such that rivers cannot quench,

   Nor ought but love from thee, give recompense.

Thy love is such I can no way repay,

   The heavens reward thee manifold, I pray.

Then while we live, in love let's so persever,

   That when we live no more, we may live ever.

ABOUT THE TEXT

Considered America's first poet, Anne Bradstreet came to the New World from England at the age of eighteen and was among the first settlers of Massachusetts Bay Colony. Bradstreet's first efforts at poetry were skillful imitations of the most respected English Puritan poets of the day. As the years passed, however, Bradstreet found her own voice. In the 1600s, it was virtually unheard of for a Puritan woman to write poetry. But Anne Bradstreet wrote moving verses, such as "To My Dear and Loving Husband," about her faith, her family, and her life in New England. She began a tradition of independent, creative expression that remains strong in America today.

*A whisper is shared in LOVERS MEETING by artist John Absolon. Photo from
The Cummer Museum of Art and Gardens, Jacksonville/Superstock.*

May Morning

Henry David Thoreau

The school boy loitered on his way to school,

Scorning to live so rare a day by rule.

So mild the air a pleasure 'twas to breathe,

For what seems heaven above was earth beneath.

Soured neighbors chatted by the garden pale,

Nor quarreled who should drive the needed nail—

The most unsocial made new friends that day,

As when the sun shines husbandmen make hay.

How long I slept I know not, but at last

I felt my consciousness returning fast,

For Zephyr rustled past with leafy tread,

And heedlessly with one heel grazed my head.

My eyelids opened on a field of blue,

For close above a nodding violet grew,

A part of heaven it seemed, which one could scent,

Its blue commingling with the firmament.

*This field in Vashon Island, Washington, is filled with
baby-blue-eyes. Photo by Mary Liz Austin.*

Love Notes

Beverly J. Anderson

God speaks in countless ways in spring:
The earth reborn, the birds on wing,
The sunshine warm, the blossoming trees,
The greening hills, the scented breeze.

Oh, how I love each flower gay
That's spread across the hills today;
And in the meadows fair and bright
These petaled beauties bring delight.

A family of new ducklings warms themselves on a log.
Photo by Gary Randall/FPG International.

Each garden is a work of art
With colors that uplift the heart—
The vivid tulips reaching up
Catch golden sunbeams in a cup.

The waltzing yellow daffodils
Don cheery bonnets trimmed with frills;
The hyacinths in pastel dress:
A vision of sheer loveliness.

The lilacs robed in purple hue,
The dainty violets, pansies too,
In gardens and upon the hills,
In woodlands and in windowsills,

In fields and valleys an array
Of floral beauty's on display;
And in each springtime wonder grand
I see a love note from God's hand.

Above: This family shot was sent to us by Kathryn M. Sattler of Whittier, California. Kathryn has seven grandchildren and eleven great-grandchildren, eight of whom are pictured here with Kathryn. She definitely never lacks someone to love!

Right: Six-month-old Rafael Silk Lee is ready for a luau in her hometown of Honolulu, Hawaii. The picture was sent to us by Rafael's proud grandmother, Lois Miller of Greenville, Ohio. Lois tells us that since she doesn't get to Honolulu very often, she couldn't wait to see Rafael in the pages of *Ideals!*

Far Right: Sandra Remmert of Champaign, Illinois, wanted to share with *Ideals* this picture of granddaughter Hannah Rae Remmert, age three and a half. Hannah is happily playing dress up in a bridal gown made just for her by Grandmother Sandra.

Thank you Kathryn M. Sattler, Sandra Remmert, Lois Miller, and Anna-Marie Mozzicato for sharing your family photographs with *Ideals*. We hope to hear from other readers who would like to share snapshots with the *Ideals* family. Please include a self-addressed, stamped envelope if you would like the photos returned. Keep your original photographs for safekeeping and send duplicate photos along with your name, address, and telephone number to:

READERS' FORUM
IDEALS PUBLICATIONS INC.
P.O. BOX 305300
NASHVILLE, TENNESSEE 37230

Above: Anna-Marie Mozzicato of Ft. Myers, Florida, sent us this snapshot of her seven-month-old granddaughter Dakotah Katherine Boone. Anna-Marie says Dakotah, who lives in Round Rock, Texas, is a "little ray of Texas sunshine." We agree!

ideals

Publisher, Patricia A. Pingry
Editor, Michelle Prater Burke
Prepress Manager, Eve DeGrie
Designer, Peggy Murphy-Jones
Copy Editor, Kristi Richardson
Editorial Assistant, Christine M. Landry
Contributing Editors, Lansing Christman, Deana Deck, Pamela Kennedy, Patrick McRae, Nancy Skarmeas

ACKNOWLEDGMENTS

DICKINSON, EMILY. "Nature the gentlest mother is." Reprinted by permission of the publishers and the Trustees of Amherst College from *The Poems of Emily Dickinson*, Thomas H. Johnson, ed., Cambridge, Mass.: The Belknap Press of Harvard University Press, copyright © 1951, 1955, 1979, 1983 by the President and Fellows of Harvard College. HOLMES, MARJORIE. "Washday at Dawn" from *You and I and Yesterday*. Reprinted by permission of the author. JAQUES, EDNA. "Earth's Fragrance" from *Hills of Home*. Published in Canada by Thomas Allen & Son Limited. MURTON, JESSIE WILMORE. "Lilac Time" from *The Shining Thread*. Printed by courtesy of Pacific Press Publishing Association, Inc. RICHARDSON, ISLA PASCHAL. "Rain at Night" from *My Heart Waketh*. Reprinted by permission of Branden Publishing Company, Boston. TREMBLE, STELLA CRAFT. "A Waking World" from *Wind in the Reed*. Reprinted by permission of Branden Publishing Company, Boston.

Prayer *for* Another Spring

Earle J. Grant

Lord, may I live until another spring,

I pray, that I might hold each lovely thing

That Thou dost bestow in my heart's embrace:

The pink of arbutus and dogwood-lace,

A redbud trailing rubies down the lane;

The forsythia dripping golden rain.

I wish to see once more the loveliness

Of violets that always come to dress

The woods in purple, and my greening hill

Frosted with windflowers—if it be Thy will.